LANCASHIRE
IN THE 20's AND 30's
from old photographs

LANCASHIRE

IN THE 20's AND 30's

from old photographs

C. E. Makepeace

B. T. BATSFORD LTD   LONDON

Frontispiece
1. *Pupils from Varna Street School, Openshaw, Manchester on their way to school to be evacuated in September 1939*

First published 1977
Reprinted 1984, 1985
Copyright © C. E. Makepeace 1977

Phototypeset by Tradespools Ltd, Frome, Somerset
Printed and bound in Great Britain by
Anchor Brendon Ltd, Tiptree, Essex
for the Publishers, B. T. Batsford Ltd
4 Fitzhardinge Street, London W1H 0AH

ISBN 0 7134 0439 6

Contents

ACKNOWLEDGEMENTS

Many of the photographs in this volume have come from collections i
Lancashire's public libraries. I should like to express my gratitude t
the staffs of these libraries for their assistance on my visits to then
Special thanks should go to the staff of Manchester Local Histor
Library for their help. I should also like to thank the publishers fc
their assistance and the following for their individual help: A. J. Pas
Mrs A. Linkman, Miss G. Howarth, D. Rendall, who produced man
of the prints used in this work, Miss J. Tarbuck and Miss D. Winte
bottom. I should especially like to thank my wife, Hilary, for he
encouragement and help. Individual photographs come from th
following libraries and sources:
Accrington, 79; Bacup 111; Barrow-in-Furness 29, 30, 106; Black
burn 43; Bolton 33; Bootle 50, 90, 92; Burnley 66; Bury 83; Hug
Cavendish 81; Chorley 34; Colne 3, 17; Crosby 76, 94; Daily Mail 1,
23, 24, 36, 49, 51, 61, 78; Darwen 39, 42, 95; R. Dunning 28, 57, 72, 8
96, 109; Eccles 93; Fleetwood 32, 112; Horwich 47; Lancaster Museum
11, 13, 118; Lancashire Evening Post 97; Leigh 5, 15, 45, 46, 68, 8
Liverpool Daily Post 115; Liverpool 14, 41, 108, 114; Mancheste
Evening News 52, 56; Manchester Guardian 26, 31, 54; Mancheste
6, 16, 18, 20, 21, 22, 25, 27, 35, 40, 60, 62, 69, 70, 75, 87, 105, 113, 11
117, 120; Mersey Docks and Harbour Board 19; Morecombe Visitc
101; Nelson 4, 48, 53, 100, 119; Platt Hall Costume Gallery, Mancheste
80, Radio Times Hulton Picture Library 8, 37, 64, 71, 88, 98, 99, 10
Radcliffe 89, 110; Rawtenstall 73; Rochdale 67, 84; Salford 63; Soutl
port 10, 74, 77, 91, 103, 107; St Anne's on Sea 104; Stretford 12
Swinton 44, 55, 58, 59; Warrington 9; Widnes 86, Wigan 2; Miss L
Wilcockson 65; Wood Street Mission, Manchester 38.

In all cases I have tried to trace the owners of the copyright an
apologise if I have inadvertently infringed this in any way.

Introduction

THE PERIOD 1918 to 1939 was one when Lancashire, like the rest of the United Kingdom, began the long process of finding a new role in a radically different world. Not only had the map of Europe been re-drawn by the Treaty of Versailles in 1919, but the war had enabled other nations, who could be regarded as Britain's competitors in the field of trade and commerce, to develop their own industries and to start to capture markets that for many years had been regarded as British. At home, the switch from a war economy to a peace-time one was achieved very quickly and many thousands of demobilised ex-servicemen returned home to jobs that they had occupied before the outbreak of war. Many came back from the war believing that things would be better than before it and in this belief they were encouraged by a speech delivered by the war-time Prime Minister, David Lloyd George, on 24 November 1918, in which he asked the question, 'What is our task?' and gave the answer, 'To make Britain a fit country for heroes to live in'. Immediately after the war there had been an economic boom, but this quickly turned into depression with soaring unemployment, and unrest, not only in industry but also in the political field. Tempers flared and violence resulted in some areas. It was as a result of the threat of violence from various political factions that Manchester City Council sought to introduce a bill into Parliament to ban the wearing of political uniforms. Although Manchester was refused permission for such a bill, the national government reacted quickly and introduced its own bill, which was quickly passed by Parliament and went onto the statute book in 1935.

During the depression of the 'twenties and 'thirties, Lancashire, in common with other areas that relied on long-established or heavy industries for their pre-war prosperity, was amongst the worst affected, with unemployment constantly above 10% of the insured population. Despite this, the population of Lancashire continued to increase, although at a much slower rate than it had previously done. In 1921, the population was 4,932,951 of whom over $1\frac{1}{2}$ million lived either in Liverpool or Manchester and less than $\frac{1}{2}$ million in the rural areas of the county. By 1931, the population had increased by 2.2% to over 5 million with the increase being found in the areas where newer, lighter industries were located—in the south-western half of the county in places like St Helens, whose population rose between 1921 and 1931 by over 4,000 to 106,793 inhabitants. Liverpool was the county's largest city with 805,046 residents in 1921 and 855,539 in 1931. Manchester was the second largest city with a population of 735,774 in 1921 and of 766,333 in 1931. Liverpool and Manchester were considerably larger than the remaining towns of Lancashire, the third largest being Salford whose population was in the region of 230,000. Between 1921 and 1931, many towns in north and east Lancashire suffered from either a declining population or a static one. Burnley's population declined from 103,186 in 1921 to 98,259 in 1931 whilst that of Barrow-in-Furness fell from 72,244 to 66,366. During the same period Rochdale and Bootle were both able to keep a relatively static population, around 90,000 and 76,000 respectively.

The areas which suffered from a declining population were also those which had suffered most from the contraction in world trade and

Previous page
2. *The banks of the Liverpool-Leeds Canal at Wigan in the 1930s. The remains of 'Wigan Pier' are in the background on the opposite bank*

3. *Children in Duerden's Yard, Waterside, Colne, 1935*

ibsequent depression, for the main employers of labour were firms
which were engaged in either cotton or engineering or were involved in
oal mining. In the cotton textile areas, after an initial post-war boom,
when there was much re-capitalisation and reconstruction of mill
finances, the industry went through very difficult times. The main
sufferers were those mills engaged in the production of the cheaper
quality cloths, which could be made overseas in countries like India
and Japan as little skill was required and lower transport costs were
incurred as the raw material was grown locally. In Japan, Egypt and
India there was a ready market for the home-produced cotton cloth at
very low prices. It was precisely these markets that part of the Lancashire textile industry had supplied before 1914, which part now found

itself in such difficulties. Those mills engaged in the manufacture of the more expensive cloths recovered some of their lost markets after the initial down-turn of trade, but overall, between 1921 and 1928, there was a 38% decrease in cotton exports from Lancashire.

The decline in output from the cotton mills resulted in high levels of unemployment. The cotton manufacturing areas of Lancashire consistently returned some of the highest figures in the whole county. For example, in January 1921, Bacup had 22% of its insured population out of work compared with an average of 12.9% for the whole county and in July 1933 Rawtenstall had an unemployment rate amongst its insured working population of 69.5% whilst the county average was 23.3%. So certain were the leaders of both sides of industry that foreign competition was the root cause of the depression that when Gandhi visited Lancashire in September 1931, they took the opportunity to meet him and put their case, but they got little comfort as Gandhi argued that India should employ its own labour to produce the country's needs.

With such high unemployment figures, it is obvious that the textile industry was not the only industry to suffer from the depression. Lancashire had a wide variety of industries ranging from coal mining to engineering and glass manufacturing. Some firms were unable to survive and they simply closed down, adding to an already serious situation, whilst others were just able to keep solvent. For example, Beyer Peacock's locomotive works at Gorton was kept in existence by an order from Russia and by the management bringing its employees in on a rota basis, thus enabling the skilled work force to be kept together and everyone to have a little work. In another field, the number of coal mines in Lancashire fell from 286 in 1921 to 198 in 1930—a drop of almost a third—but production per miner rose from 180 tons a year in 1922 to 193 in 1930. Despite this, Lancashire's contribution to national coal production fell from 7.3% to 6.3% between 1922 and 1930.

Although central government attempted to tidy up the unemployment relief system, it was not totally successful and much was left to local councils and voluntary organisations to try and deal with the situation. One method adopted was the provision of public works such as the building of new roads and reconstructing of others. For example, Heywood Old Road at Middleton was widened and improved in the 1920s by the unemployed of the town. In the 'thirties, with unemployment at a much higher level, clubs were established in towns where the unemployed could gather and spend their days in useful occupations such as rug making. Manchester even had a newspaper called *Roundabout* which was intended to keep high the morale of those out of work and encourage them to occupy their time profitably. Not that local schemes to help the unemployed went smoothly. The Manchester papers of 1933 were full of complaints about the way Manchester's unemployed club was being administered, but this did not last and by 1935, the complaints had disappeared from the papers.

Despite unemployment, reduced wages and unrest, the face of Lancashire began to change more rapidly than ever before. Large areas of sub-standard housing were swept away in slum clearance programmes and their residents rehoused in new council houses built under various

Acts of Parliament passed between 1919 and 1936. Some authorities used private builders to do the work whilst others established their own direct works department to do the work. Even the small authorities did their share of the work; for example, Prestwich built 1,086 houses during the inter-war period.

Although the provision of council homes was a new form of local government expenditure, many cuts were simultaneously made in other areas. Libraries were compelled to reduce the amount of non-book material they acquired with the result that gaps exist in collections of local material, and it is only recently that steps have been taken to attempt to fill them. For example, photographic records that now exist in libraries have come from private individuals, corporation departments and the press and were rarely specifically taken for the library.

Not only did changes start to alter the face of the county, but they also affected the status of some local authorities. Proposals were put forward for merging authorities and establishing a two-tier system of local government. Places like Prestwich, Crosby, Swinton and Stretford were afraid they would lose their independence so they sought and achieved borough status in the 1930s. Some authorities did succeed in enlarging their areas: Accrington absorbed Huncoat in 1929 whilst Manchester took a large bite out of North Cheshire for its Wythenshawe estate in 1931.

Changes also took place in the forms of transport available to Lancastrians between the wars. The private motor car enabled more and more people to travel at their own convenience whilst the railways turned to electrification as their means of maintaining competitiveness with the roads. However, it was in the form of air transport that the greatest revolution took place. In 1929 Manchester became the first provincial town with a direct, regular air link with London. The original Manchester airport was merely a field at Rackhouse Wythenshawe, but it soon moved to a purpose-built site at Barton, where it remained until 1938 when the present Ringway Airport was opened. Most flights that operated from Manchester were internal. International flights started when K.L.M. introduced a service between Manchester and Amsterdam via Hull. The development of further continental connections was held up by the outbreak of war in 1939. Liverpool too had its own airport providing a direct service between Lancashire and the Isle of Man. The cost of flying, however, was such that only a very limited number of people could benefit.

One tradition which continued was the Annual Wakes Week when the whole town closed down for the annual holiday. The Lancashire coast was especially popular with holidaymakers not only from Lancashire, but from all parts of the country. In 1939, Blackpool estimated that it received seven million visitors during the holiday season. The Pennines were a popular venue for those who preferred to walk and enjoy the peace of the hills. The problem of public access to the moors created much bitterness between the residents of the industrial towns and the gamekeepers and landowners. Pitched battles were sometimes fought and mass trespasses organised to support the case of those who argued that the moors were free for everyone to use, not only the wealthy few.

The collection of statistics increased between the wars. For the first time it is possible to discover what the average family spent on items like food, entertainment and rent. In the late 1930s the average family in Lancashire is calculated to have spent 2s 10d a week on bread 2s 3d on mutton and lamb and 2s 1d on fresh fish. The average weekly expenditure was given as 83s 6d. per family. This was broken down as follows: rent and rates 10s 8d, 33s 3d on food, 7s 10d on clothing, 6s 7d on fuel and light and 25s 2d on other items such as entertainment, holidays and subscriptions.

Sport in Lancashire went through a relatively successful period between the wars. The First Division Championship of the Football League was won on seven occasions by Lancashire Clubs—Everton winning it twice, and the F.A. Cup on seven occasions—Bolton winning it three times between 1918 and 1939. On the cricket field, Lancashire were county champions 1926–28, 1930 and 1934.

The selection of photographs has been made in order to give an overall impression of life in the county between the wars. The subjects covered have, however, been to some extent limited by what photographs have survived and by constraints on the space available.

The Return of Peace

Previous page
4. *Formal celebrations to mark the return of peace were held in the summer of 1919 when many of those who had joined the forces had been discharged and prisoners-of-war repatriated. In Radcliffe, a large bonfire was built and an effigy of the Kaiser placed at the top whilst in Nelson, the local cricket ground, shown in the photograph, was the setting for a thanksgiving service on 3 August*

5. *Repatriated prisoners-of-war and their wives at a dinner given in Leigh in 1919 to mark their return home*

6. *The Armistice Day ceremony in Manchester in 1933. It took place in Albert Square as the area around the Cenotaph in St Peter's Square was too small for the crowds who attended*

Street Scenes

Below
7. *Oxford Street, Manchester about 1937, shortly before a one-way system was introduced along that section of road*

Right
8. *Christmas shoppers on Lord Street, Southport in 1931*

Right, below
9. *Traffic converging on Market Gate, Warrington in the early 1920s*

10. *The frontage of Muirhead and Willcock's shop, Chapel Street, Southport in the early 1920s*

11. *Kiln Lane, Lancaster, 1920*

2. *William Valentine's newsagents shop on King Street, Stretford in 1929. Amongst the advertisements for popular newspapers is a billboard advertising coach trips to Lytham St Annes and Blackpool on Wednesdays, Saturdays and Sundays*

3. *Cable Street, Lancaster in 1927*

14. *Market Street, Liverpool, from the corner of Roe Street and Brythen Street in 1934, showing the open-air dog market held on Saturdays*

15. *Bengal Street, Leigh, looking from Vicarage Square towards Railway Street, 1932*

16. *Two farm workers on Bentley Hall Road, Walshaw, near Bury (15 August 1939)*

17. *Lister Street, Colne, in June 1932. Washing hanging across the street was often an indication of the existence of back-to-back housing, of which there were many examples in Lancashire*

eft

8. A scissor grinder in Lancashire 1932. The wheel served a double rpose: it could be used to trundle the uipment from door to door as well to turn the grindstone

The Pier Head and Liver ilding, Liverpool from the bridge of rans-Atlantic liner in 1936

Rectory Lane, Prestwich, 1938, king towards Bury New Road

21. *A barrow boy's cart on Market Street, Manchester, 1 July 1939*

22. *Bull's Head Yard, Manchester in November 1936. England won the test match against Australia referred to on the posters by 322 runs*

Cleminson Street, Salford, 1929

At Work

left

4. *Customers in Mrs Spring's*
general store, 180 Chester Road,
Manchester in 1939 when the price of a
loaf of bread was about 4½d. Mrs
Spring owned the shop from around
1918 until the early 1950s

25. *Cotton winding at a Bolton mill*
in December 1927

6.   *Miners leaving the pit head at Astley Green Colliery in October 1934 after completing their shift underground. The winding engine at Astley Green was one of the largest in the world. Built by Yates and Thom of Blackburn, the tandem compound engine was capable of raising 8 tons of coal 2,628 feet to the surface in 60 seconds—a maximum rope speed of 2 feet per second*

7.   *Women grading coal at one of the collieries owned by the Wigan Coal and Iron Company, December 1932*

28. *Aircraft production at A. V. Roe's Manchester factory in 1933. The aircraft under production is not identified, but could be one of an order for 300 Tudors placed by the government*

29. *Machining material for the balloon of an airship at the Vicker's works. Walney Island, Barrow-in-Furness around 1918*

30. *The scene at a launching of a new ship at Vicker's shipyard, Barrow-in-Furness, in the late 1930s when much of the production was directed towards rearmament*

1. *The manufacture of wireless
valves at Ferranti's works,
Manchester, November 1934*

32. *Fleetwood was one of the main centres of the Lancashire fishing industry. On 14 October 1927, the golden jubilee of the opening of the Wyre Dock was celebrated. Here, Sir Josiah Stamp, Chairman of the L.M.S. Railway is being presented with a box of kippers by fish dock workers wearing traditional costume.*

33. *Men using specially constructed wheelbarrows moving part of the stock of Bolton Central Library to new premises in 1938*

34. *A livestock class at Chorley Show, 1938*

35. *Slippers and sandals were the main products of Lancashire's footwear industry centred on the Rossendale Valley. The photograph was taken in December 1927 when between 6,000 and 7,000 people were thus employed*

36. *A visit of the Salvation Army soup kitchen to the Manchester poor in December 1930*

37. *Part of the floor of the Royal Exchange, Manchester on a day of High 'Change in the 1930s*

38. *Father Christmas distributing presents to children at Wood Street Mission, Manchester, in the early 1930s. The presents were paid for out of donations to the Mission*

39. *A cookery class at Darwen Social Service Centre (1935)*

Children

Left

40. Seaside camps for children from the poorer quarters of Lancashire's urban areas had been regular events from the mid-1880s. Boys from Manchester and Salford are here seen peeling potatoes at a camp at Birkdale during the summer of 1939

41. Shoe blacks around the Patrick Byrne Fountain at the top of Byrom Street, Liverpool, December 1938

42. Hand tennis at Darwen Social Service Centre, 1936

43. *At the Blackburn Public Library 1920*

44. *For children brought up in the smoky towns and cities of Lancashire, lung conditions were common. To combat this, open-air schools were established where children could be kept out of doors in a reasonably pollution-free atmosphere as long as possible. The photograph is of Barton Road Open Air School, Swinton about 1934*

45. *The Flash near Leigh, with Plank Lane Colliery, Bickershaw in the background*

46. *At the opening of the Watson Playing Fields, Leigh in May 1932*

47. *A class in a Horwich school in the late 1920s*

48. *Second-year school children at Barrowford, near Nelson, dressed in traditional costume, dancing round the maypole (1923)*

Social Conditions

Previous page
49. *The arrest of unemployed, Bexley Square, Salford after a demonstration over the level of unemployment, October 1931*

50. *Irlam Road Unemployed Club, Bootle in 1933 where those unable to find work could spend their days making rugs and rush-matting*

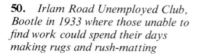

51. *Unemployed men from Lancashire marching to London in October 1936 to join up with the Jarrow marchers*

52. *The Salvation Army provided free coffee for the unemployed waiting outside the Labour Exchange in Manchester*

3. *Weavers protesting about wage
cuts marching along Carr Road,
Nelson in 1936*

54. *A lorry taking workers into central Manchester passing along Stockport Road on 6 May 1926 during the General Strike*

5. *A backyard of a slum house in Swinton photographed by the Medical Officer of Health about 1935 as part of his programme of slum clearance. The washing on the line was deliberately pushed up to show how little yard space was available*

6. *Picking coal on a south Lancashire slag heap in the 1920s*

57. *Pickets outside a Burnley mill in October 1931*

58. *Caravans at the rear of Longshawe Buildings, Potter Street, Swinton around 1935*

59. *Bedding being aired over coke braziers at the Destructor Plant, Swinton in 1934 or 1935 after fumigation by cyanide fumes to kill any infestation. The owners of the bedding were being moved from condemned slum housing to new council houses*

0. *Queuing for water, Dalton*
Street, Salford after a water main had
burst, 1938

61. *Javelin throwing at a camp for the unemployed at Ulveston in 1939. The camp was organised by the Lancashire and Cheshire Community Council and replaced camps at Bowness and Edale. During 1939 over 1,000 men each paid 7/6d for a week at the camp*

62. *Gypsies near Belle Vue, Manchester, 1932*

Leisure and Pleasure

Previous page
63. *Salford playing Huddersfield at Rugby League in 1937, a match which Salford won by 38 points to 8*

64. *Holiday crowds at an amusement stall, Blackpool (1939)*

5. *Charabanc trips were increasingly popular. The charabanc in the photograph was owned by Wilcockson Brothers of Middleton Junction*

6. *Burnley Wakes Fair in 1924 in the town's Cattle Market*

67. *Mr W. S. Schofield of Littleborough with his knurr-and-spell frame*

68. *A wireless discussion group at Leigh Library in November 1930*

69. *Matt Busby of Liverpool F.C. and Sam Langford of Manchester City F.C. giving a lesson in ball control to Sam's son, Len, at the Manchester University Athletic Ground, Fallowfield, 1937*

70. *Players of Lancashire County Cricket Club prepare for the 1937 season at Old Trafford, Stretford under their coach, Harry Makepeace*

71. *At the 1926 Grand National,*
Aintree

72. *A meeting at Aintree in the 1930s*

73. *Alderman James Taylor of Waterfoot, a keen follower of the Bacup, Rossendale and Holcombe Hounds for 75 years, at the New Inn, Walmesley in January 1934*

74. *Southport had two important golf courses. In 1933 the Dunlop Professional Golf Tournament was played over the Southport and Ainsdale course. Henry Cotton is here seen on the 18th green*

75. *A close measure during the qualifying rounds for the Meggatt Bowl held at the Manchester Ice Palace during late March and early April 1938. The tournament was the last major curling event of the season and attracted entries from all over the north of England, including the team from Preston shown in the photograph*

76. *Litherland Prize Band, 1926*

77. *Arthur Jacobson playing at the Floral Hall, Southport about 1935*

78. *The cast of the new farce,* The Night of the Garter, *arrive at London Road Station, Manchester, prior to the show's opening at the Opera House on 1 August 1932. From left to right:* Angela Baddeley, Miss Brooks, Sydney Howard, Jane Welsh, Austin Melford.

79. *Hiking was popular between 1918 and 1939. People from Lancashire's industrial towns sometimes fought battles with the gamekeepers in the Pennines to secure the right of public access. These hikers are near Warmden Reservoir near Accrington in August 1929*

80. *A wedding group at Ince-in-Makerfield in 1927*

81. *Queen Mary visits Holker Hall*

Public Events

2. *A street in Hulme, Manchester
ecorated to celebrate the coronation
f George VI in 1937*

3. *The Prince of Wales, later Duke
f Windsor, talking to disabled
x-servicemen at Bury in 1921 during
 four-day visit to the north-west*

4. *One of the leading entertainers
etween the wars was Rochdale's
racie Fields, shown in the photograph
eing received by the mayor, Mrs J.
uckworth, after being given the
eedom of Rochdale (1939)*

85. *Ox-roasting at Tyldesley in October 1925*

86. *The Mayor of Widnes welcoming George V to Widnes on 8 July 1925. The King had stayed the previous night at Knowsley Hall, near Liverpool before visiting the Royal Agricultural Show at Chester*

87. *Presentation of the freedom of the City of Manchester to C. P. Scott in 1936*

88. *'Reynoldstown'; winner of the 1935 Grand National*

89. *Ducking the mock 'Mayor' of Ringley in the Manchester, Bolton and Bury Canal, 1925*

90. *One of the floats entered in the Bootle May Day Carnival, 1936*

91. *Spectators at Crossens Summer Festival in 1924*

92. *Margery Roscoe, Bootle May Queen for 1934, with her retinue on the way to the throne at May Queen celebrations*

93. *Children from King Street Mission, Eccles, taking part in the Whit Walk on the Thursday after Whit Sunday 1938 (Golden Jubilee Year). Many Lancashire towns had walks during the Whitsuntide period with different denominations walking on different days. In Manchester, the Anglicans walked on Whit Monday, the Catholics on the following Friday.*

94. *Lord Derby being received by the Charter Mayor of Crosby at Seaforth Sands railway station in 1937 when he came to deliver the official documents creating Crosby a borough*

95. *Between 25 and 27 September 1931, Spring Valley Garden Village near Darwen had the Indian nationalist leader Mahatma Gandhi as a visitor. During his private visit to the area, Gandhi called on the Mayor of Darwen and had discussions with both sides of the Lancashire textile industry, who were worried about the effect on local employment of India's emergent industry*

96. *Ramsey Macdonald, Labour Prime Minister, laying the foundation stone of Manchester Central Library 1930. The circular-shaped building was designed by Vincent Harris and was opened by George V in 1934. The building provided Manchester Public Libraries with its first purpose-built headquarters. Previously it had occupied redundant buildings and from 1912, huts in Piccadilly*

97. *Every 20 years Preston celebrates the granting of the borough's Key Charter in the twelfth century. The photograph shows part of one of the many processions that took place during the 1922 Guild*

At the Seaside

101. *The paddling pool on the front at Morecombe in the 1930s*

02. *Easter holidaymakers at*
Morecombe in 1934

103. *Holidaymakers at the Ainsdale
Bathing Centre, Southport in either
1938 or 1939*

104. *St Anne's pier orchestra 1928*

Getting About

Previous page
105. *The East Lancashire Road, linking Liverpool and Manchester and avoiding the intermediate towns, was opened in July 1934 by George V. Although it did not reduce the mileage between the cities, it considerably shortened the journey time*

Right
107. *The Mayor welcoming the famous airwoman Amy Johnson to Southport in 1930*

106. *The airship R80 at her moorings on Walney Island after completion by Vickers of Barrow-in-Furness*

Right, below
108. *M.V.* Britannic *in March 1931 about to leave Lancashire's main port, Liverpool, on her maiden voyage*

111. *The last tram between Haslingden and Accrington (1930)*

Left, above
109. *Oxford Road Station, Manchester, in the early afternoon of 11 May 1931, showing one of the newly introduced electric trains serving the important Manchester to Altrincham commuter route and intended to compete more effectively with road transport*

Left
110. *Nob End Locks at Little Lever on the Manchester, Bolton and Bury Canal*

112. *Fleetwood lifeboat during a practice launch on the River Wyre*

113. *The Port of Manchester stretching along the banks of the Manchester Ship Canal from Eastham to Manchester was Liverpool's greatest rival as Lancashire's main port. In the 10 years, 1918 to 1928, tonnage handled by the canal rose from 3½ million to almost 6½ million tons despite the fact that the size of vessels which could use the port was restricted*

114. *Waiting for the ferry to cross the River Mersey from Liverpool to Birkenhead about 1920. Until the opening of the Mersey Tunnel, the ferry was the only direct link between the two towns*

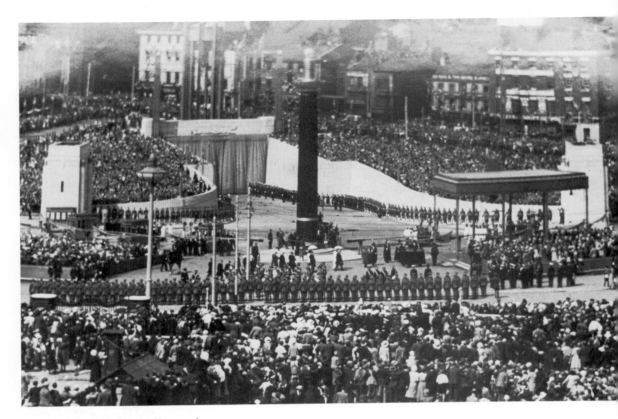

115. *In July 1934 George V opened the Mersey Tunnel linking Liverpool with Birkenhead by road for the first time*

The Approach of War

Previous page
116. *Children from Chorlton Park
School, Manchester walking in
crocodile along Barlow Moor Road to
Chorlton Station to be evacuated,
2 September 1939*

117. *Evacuation instructions posted in the playground of a south Manchester school on 27 August 1939*

118. *Volunteers arriving at Bowerham Barracks, Lancaster in September 1939 to join the King's Own Royal Regiment (Lancaster)*

119. *A pacifist float entered for a gala procession organised by Reedymere Hospital, Nelson in the mid 1930s. The lady standing on the right is Mrs J. Cooper J.P., a former suffragette who had visited Germany as a member of the International Women's Committee against War and Fascism*

120. *The first delivery of Anderson
air-raid shelters to a Manchester
council house estate in 1939*